D0111404

"Morgan Parker's second book of poetry, *There Are More Beautiful Things Than Beyoncé*, isn't just the most ferocious collection to be published this year. It's also an antidote to the culture of hate and white supremacy reincarnated by our new administration. . . . It's part psychic excavation, part historical exorcism. Having watched Nina Simone in concert on YouTube most of my adult life, I've finally found an experience to compare that to."

—INTERVIEW

"Parker's poems brings heat to the art of Mickalene Thomas, the racial politics of Barack Obama's presidency, the body politics of Beyoncé, and the danger of moving through America in a black body: 'I walk into a bar. / I drink a lot of wine and kiss a Black man on his beard. / I do whatever I want because I could die any minute. / I don't mean YOLO I mean they are hunting me.'"

—TIME

"Easily one of the most compelling poetry collections of the past few years, *There Are More Beautiful Things Than Beyoncé* is fresh, unexpected, and intimate; an equally devastating and uplifting exploration of black womanhood; and a tender and lovely celebration of life."

—SHONDALAND

"Parker's poetry is a sledgehammer covered in silk, exposing black women's vulnerability and power and underscoring what it means to be magical and in pain."

—BUZZFEED

"The first thing you have to understand is that Morgan Parker is one of the most fascinating poets working today. She writes poems that are clever, beautiful, political, playful, breathtaking. . . . I know I'm excited to see what happens and thrilled to watch Parker continue killing it on the page."

—BOOK RIOT

"Employing fierce language and eschewing fear of unflattering light, Parker pays homage to the deep roots and collective wisdom of black womanhood. . . . Parker's poems are as flame-forged as a chain locked around soft ankles."

—PUBLISHER'S WEEKLY
Starred Review

"These words, brilliant, lovely, and sharp like a diamond, cut me deeply and left me in awe of Parker's writing. This book is an exciting contribution to the rich legacy of Black feminist art, literature, poetry, and music that daily adds more complex representations of Black American womanhood."

—BITCH

"Outstanding collection of poems. So much soul. So much intelligence in how Parker folds in cultural references and the experiences of black womanhood. Every poem will get its hooks into you. And of course, the poems about Beyoncé are the greatest because Beyoncé is our queen."

—ROXANE GAY

"There are more beautiful things than Beyoncé in these pages because, as Morgan Parker writes in poems channeling the president's wife, the Venus Hottentot, and multiple Beyoncés: 'We're everyone. We have ideas and vaginas, / history and clothes and a mother.' The kind of verve the late New York school Ted Berrigan would have called 'feminine marvelous and tough' is here, as well as the kind of vulnerability that fortifies genuine daring. This is a marvelous book. See for yourself. Morgan Parker is a fearlessly forward and forward-thinking literary star."

—TERRANCE HAYES

"There is not a more daring artist, or anyone I'd rather read in the twenty-first century, than Morgan Parker."

—KIESE LAYMON

MAGICAL NEGRO

MAGICAL NEGRO

POEMS

MORGAN PARKER

 TIN HOUSE BOOKS / Portland, Oregon & Brooklyn, New York

Published by Tin House Books, Portland, Oregon, and Brooklyn,
New York

Distributed by W. W. Norton & Company

Library of Congress Cataloging-in-Publication Data

Names: Parker, Morgan, author.
Title: Magical negro : poems / Morgan Parker.
Description: First U.S. edition. | Portland, Oregon : Tin House Books, 2018.
Identifiers: LCCN 2018041653 | ISBN 9781947793187 (pbk.)
Classification: LCC PS3616.A74547 A6 2018 | DDC 811/.6—dc23
LC record available at https://lccn.loc.gov/2018041653

First U.S. Edition 2019
Printed in the USA
Interior design by Jakob Vala

www.tinhouse.com

It was summer now and the colored people came out into the sunshine, full blown with flowers. And they shone in the streets and in the fields with their warm joy, and they glistened in their black heat, and they flung themselves free in their wide abandonment of shouting laughter.

—GERTRUDE STEIN, *Three Lives*

CONTENTS

I.
LET US NOW PRAISE FAMOUS MAGICAL NEGROES

II.
FIELD NEGRO
FIELD NOTES

III.
POPULAR NEGRO PUNCHLINES

I.
LET US NOW
PRAISE FAMOUS
MAGICAL NEGROES

I Feel Most Colored When I Am Thrown Against a Sharp White Background

after Glenn Ligon after Zora Neale Hurston

Or, I feel sharp white.
Or, colored against.
Or, I am thrown. I am against. Or, when white. I sharp. I color.
Quiet. Forget. My country is a boat.
I feel most colored when I swear to god.
I feel most colored when it is too late.
When I am captive.
The last thing on my mind is death.
I tongue elegy.
I color green because green is the color of power.
I am growing two fruits.
I feel most colored when I am thrown against the sidewalk.
It is the last time I feel colored.
Stone is the name of the fruit.
I am a man I am a man I am a woman I am a man I am a
    woman I am protected and served.
I background my country.
My country sharp in my throat.
I pay taxes and I am a child and I grow into a bright
    fleshy fruit.
White bites: I stain the uniform.
I am thrown black typeface in a headline with no name.
Or, no one hears me.

I am thrown bone, "Unarmed."

I feel most colored when my weapon is I.

When I get what I deserve.

When I can't breathe.

When on television I shuffle and widen my eyes.

I feel most colored when I am thrown against a mattress,
     my tits my waist my ankles buried in.

White ash. Everyone claps.

I feel most colored when I am the punchline. When I am
     the trigger.

In the dawn, putrid yellow, I know what I am being told.

My country pisses on my grave.

My country bigger than god.

Elegy my country.

I feel most colored when I am collecting dust.

When I am impatient and sick. They use us to distract us.

My ears leak violet petals.

I sharpen them. I sharpen them again.

Everyone claps.

Magical Negro #217: Diana Ross Finishing a Rib in Alabama, 1990s

Since I thought I'd be dead
by now everything
I do is fucking perfect walking wreck
reckless and men
I suck their bones until they're perfect
I don't sleep with accolades I don't get touched
in the night all men do is cry
and ask me to be their mama I can't
get a decent fuck to save my
when I think about their feelings I don't care
It's cool it's cool come to mama there is so much
death here she is casual and almost fragrant like
the word *kill* doesn't sound as bad as it is
All my friends are sisters and husbands I'm afraid
to be uncharted I want an empire in my teeth but I can't
be bothered to wear anything but silk
I have grown up less mysterious than my myth
All men do is think I'm looking at them
When I think about them tasting me I don't
I mean don't Google my tits when you can just
Unfortunately I have a body and I'm the only
one in charge of it you know what I eat the bones too
I'm in the world I'm in the world
nobody cares where I came from

Everything Will Be Taken Away

after Adrian Piper

You can't stop mourning
everything all the time.

The '90s, the black Maxima with a tail,
CD wrappers, proximity to the earth.

Glamour and sweating in your sheets.
Speaking tongues. Men, even.

You are a woman now
but you have always had skin.

Here are some ways in which
you are not free: the interiors

are all wrong, you are a drought
sprawling. When you see god

you don't like what you see.
It is never enough to be born

again and again.

You like it at church when
strangers hold your hand.

You have a mouth men bless.
You look good enough to bury.

Magical Negro #3: The Strong Black Woman

She likes it rough. When you open her up through the
    mouth hole, the dumb
cunt hole. You could stomp around in there. It's fine. She
    won't feel nothing.

That played-out scene she loves so much so she can feel like
    she got a dick:
Angela Bassett at the end of the movie smoking
    a cigarette, smug bitch burning
our cities down, cleavage always only a tease, with a face
    like Can I help you.
Yes, bitch, you can. You can strip down to tears and dry cum.
    You can be
more naked.

Stop crying. I'll give you something to cry about.

She thinks she's better. She think she cute. She's holding out.
She is nothing to hold. She is no one to worship.

Inventory of her body: hair she cut to look like a man,
   too-dark nipples,
the way she waves those tits around, asking for it. She's
   always crying.
That uppity face. Holy grail pussy, a mountain peak.
   Her pussy self-defense.
A lack of serotonin. A lack of vulnerability. No chill. Nothing
   real.
No need to have her back because she don't have one. Just
   a mountain
in a dark blue wilderness. She aches from the captivity.

The High Priestess of Soul's Sunday
Morning Visit to the Wall of Respect

The Impressionism wing strikes me as too
dainty for my mood, except for one oil painting
by Gustave Caillebotte, *Calf's Head and Ox Tongue*,
which is described in the wall text as
"visually unpleasant." A bust of an African woman
bums me out. This year, I cried
at everyone's kitchen table,
I spit on the street and was late on purpose and stepped
in glass and my dog died and I saw
minuses over and over. I'll figure it out.
I let a man walk away and then
another one. It has taken me exactly this long
to realize I could have done something else.
I'm being repetitive now but do you ever
hate yourself?

AND COLD SUNSET

How I feel about you is smoking a cigarette in the rain.

I think about walking into traffic, and suddenly, your dick.

I think about a yellow line and then a road and then an animal.

And nothing rises up. And horror is a verb.

I want to forgive myself for overindulging.

Food-delivery men see me without a bra more than anyone else.

My body is an argument I did not start.

In a way I am not aware who made me.

I bow down to a deep plea.

When strangers call my name I feel like a white girl.

Skin in reverse and a quiet pussy.

Nothing helps me not think about universes.

I'm funny because I know nothing matters.

Nancy Meyers and My Dream of Whiteness

I can't be sorry
enough. I have learned
everything is urgent.
Road closings, animal lungs.
I am working hard to be
as many people as possible
before I can't.
I know my long, dark movie
is fistfuls
of gravel in a brown bottle.
My storyboards fill me
with calculated sorrow.
A full plate and burnt sage.
Dollar signs, breaking news.
I work two and three jobs.
I am honorable and brave.
The ensemble cast
whittles down.
Maybe I am a slave.
I make ends meet.
I don't get kissed.
Behold my wide smile.
Octavia Spencer cooks in a small
apartment. She serves joyfully

and doesn't eat. She wipes her palm
on her apron, forehead.
Angela Bassett is sick and tired
of being. Denzel Washington
reminds us how often
we are afraid. We get arrested.
Someone narrates.
What you look like
is sheer fabrics and ivory shells.
Alec Baldwin is smoking a joint
in the bathroom of a CEO's
birthday party. Steve Martin
tastes the goat cheese
and considers nothing.
You never get arrested.
There is no question
that god waits at the end
of your staircase curling
softly like wood-finished ribbon.
Anne Hathaway hires a decorator.
Diane Keaton makes midnight
pancakes, tops them with
lavender ice cream.
What is beautiful

does not need to be
called beautiful.
No one talks about money.
In our house, the sky
is upside down.
None of us find unlikely love.
I do not revel in my luxury.
I would rather serve than eat.
If it seems like I desire you,
you're right. I want my whole
mouth around your safety.
I want to be buried
side by side.

Whites Only

It's too late to live on a farm or in the Hamptons
or in Portland or in Brooklyn or in Oakland
or in the South I guess you'll never fill me
with blissful children and pie and entitlement
where we remark with glass eyelids how
the colors in the wheat remind us of pictures
of plantations and how that makes us want

and when I say too late I mean
we are always missing
something I guess the money or the sound
sleep of new animals who don't yet understand
what it feels like to hold
a piece of your body and know
it is the reason for everything

why some window views aren't yours
and some have the memory
of firehoses on brick and you do not
belong and it has been too late since this:
the first Atlantic baptism
growling back or
a quiet guiltless bed I guess

this floral pattern is not where we belong
I guess the radios stay on all night
and we are syrupy in our black I guess
this is a love poem
another dream of what I'm not
I guess there's no difference
between a country and a man

Magical Negro #607: Gladys Knight on the 200th Episode of *The Jeffersons*

Privilege is asking other people
to look at you. I like everything
in my apartment except me.
I mean I need to buy a toaster.
What is the point of something
that only does one thing.
My life is a kind of reality.
When I get bored, I close the window.
By the way what is a yuppie.
Here I am, two landscapes.
My tattoo artist says I'm a warrior
with pain. I tell her we can manifest
this new moon in six months.
When I'm rich I will still be Black.
You can't take the girl out of the ghetto
until she earns it, or grows up into it.
It's too much to ask to be
satisfied. Of course I sing
through the struggle. My problem is
I'm too glamorous to be seen.
How will I know when I've made it.
In the mirror will I have a face.
How long does a good thing last.
Sometimes eating a guilty salad

I become a wife.
Let me be the woman
who takes care of you.
Weezy and George in drapes
and crystal silverware.
By the way predominantly white
means white. I want to be the first
black woman to live her life
exclusively from the bathtub.
Making toast, enjoying success
despite my cultural and systemic
setbacks. I was raised to be
a nigger you can trust.
I was raised to be better
than my parents. In a small house
with a swamp cooler
I touched myself. I wanted to be
in the white mom's carpool.
My cheek against something new
and clean. I clean my apartment
when I am afraid of being
the only noise.
Everyone I know is a black man,
so I'm a black man, too.
Tragically, I win. It is a joke.

I always require explanation. See:
Life starring Martin Lawrence; or
Dope, wherein the hero must be
proof of good intention.
I am so lucky to be you.
When something dies,
I buy a new one.

Magical Negro #84: The Black Body

Give it a new verb.

Stop writing poetry.

Go outside. Make blood.

The body is a person.

The body is a person.

The body is a person.

The body is a person.

The body is a person.

Sammy Davis Jr.

There are no dressing rooms for you

                snickering in golf pants

they regret to inform

                stirring bloodies with celery stalks

a clan by any other name

                growing slowly in the courtyard

the life of a thief, a spider bite

                dead between the eyes

belly-round with misfortune

                you remember your mother, fireflies

smear your cheekbones in whiteout

                you wait outside until you are called

A fountain lights up, you forgive, again

                heaven drools with indifference

Let's Get Some Better Angels at This Party

Michael Brown, 18, due to be buried on Monday, was no angel.

—*The New York Times*

You always thought angels lived
in the dark. You didn't sleep.
Appeared at the foot of Mom's bed
covered in Nana's perfume. You saw
and kept seeing. You let them
make a crescent of your spine.
The same thing over and over.
You don't trust air. You call the ghosts
the angels your kin.
There is one who looks like your brother.
One in Nike shorts tastes sauce from
a wooden spoon and pours rum
into his brown on the stoop.
There's one who brings the weed.
There's one you call your brother.
They are already dead. They live
in the future. You see them because
you can't sleep. You feel cold.
Angels with ringtones and child support.
Angels with PhDs. One in your bed.
One calculates the tip at brunch.
One colors inside the chalk line.
One walks with you into the disco

evening, radiating purposefully.
August rain is cold. The desert
is cold. Verdicts. Seasons.
Verdicts. Night. Blood. Saliva.
A cousin of a friend of a friend who brought
a six-pack, yes, perfect, let everyone in.
Your angels fly outfits, second chances.
Handguns, candy, cigars, mothers, mothers
for your angels and children for the mothers.
They spook. They blood and sage.
And when the policemen come to break
everything   an angel
in a polo shirt answers the door, says
officers I'm sorry
I'm not

The History of Black People

1.

The saddest triptych
is our blood, trouble
passed down. A root out
on our wet stiff suits.
Everyone walks behind us.
I would rather dance
hoodwinked with the devil
than be alone. I pick
bad juju over yellow
meadow and your moon.
Florida, Kentucky hemlocks
grow in sepia glint. Red clay
everywhere. This isn't a dream—
in the beginning, red clay.

2.

The history of black people, after Jean-Michel Basquiat.
The history of black people: an allegory for
Denzel Washington's continuous battle with various
    forms of transportation.
The history of black people: a black feminist reading of
Cinderella starring Whitney Houston and Brandy.
The history of black people, or, that feeling when
Lauryn Hill is in your school choir but drops out
    right before the statewide competition.
The history of black people, a new series coming to BET
    twenty years ago.
The history of black people, an investigation.
The history of black people, a tragicomic horror film.
The history of black people, or, joy stinging pink lips.
The history of black people says me.
The history of black people goes blank.
The history of black people, adapted from white people.

3.

Single black female cries into a glass of rosé
on a Friday in April at 10:54 PM, is once again
an unpleasant movie date, makes every little thing
political, needlessly references Paula Abdul's
stint as a Laker Girl, wakes up fevering
in the dark afraid of trust, forever sucking on
a technical bad mood, imagines her bones
damned, false teeth in the grass
below her feet, is a patient culprit,
names her heart a dumb tick. Forgive us
our dissonance. We hold shame close.
A black boy's hairline finally puts us to sleep.
A sea creature shucks sand for gems.

4.

If you cut open my heart, it would be midnight
at the greatest party of all time: a miniature
Shawn Carter and Audre Lorde, feasting on difference.
Uppity Negroes and Highfalutins and Tyrones,
Rick James appearing before Judge Joe Brown,
granddaddies eating fruit over the sink, Bernie Mac
growling *America, let's talk.* I never went
to recess because I don't play. I never learned
to swim but I went swimming. I make my enemy
disease in my blood. I never believed in love.
I carry us all in me, drag my hooves in tall grass and
breathe when I'm full, bask in a real feel-good
fugitive moment. Even the sun yawns when I pray.

5.

On the first page of every library book
there's a question mark for us, backs bent out
of exclamation. We don't know any of your words
but our children have licked them up in pools
of sweat. Have you ever felt like a square peg
in a round hole? Do you sometimes dream
of a handful of Skittles sprawling on February lawn?
If our legend was allowed, it would sing
alligator's scales. It would be written in red clay.
It was an open and shut case.
It never lived to be eighteen.
This is our first and last love song.

II.
FIELD NEGRO
FIELD NOTES

Two White Girls in the African Braid Shop on Marcy and Fulton

Does it hurt. Why did you come here. What do you want.
Are you filming this. Do you live in this neighborhood.
Do you have a picture. Do you feel comfortable. Can I
ask is that a weave. Why do you feel comfortable. Is the
neighborhood treating you well. Do you read the news.
Where's your real hair. Do you like America. Are you
filming this. How much. Dollars. Did you hear about the
trial. Where are we going after this. I heard it was non-
indictment. I have been listening. Nigerian soap operas.
Praise Be to God. Did you just take a picture of me. How
do you feel about America. Is it too late. Reminds me of TV
plantations. You'll get the shoes when I have enough money.
Stop crying. Your mother loves you. Not too tight because
I am tender. Not too big because I want it to last. Why did
you come here. You know with everything that's been going
on these days. Do the radios stay on all night. Does anyone
tell a baby who they are. Who they have to keep being. How
did you sleep. Your soft kitchen. Dark nipples. This is when
we say our prayers. Women fill with infants and butter.
Who are you texting. Did we make reservations. What
language. Eyes so black they syrup. Hair so black there are
no windows. The smell of burnt rope. How long will it be.
How long do you want it. I know you. I wish I were you. I
want to drag my toes in something I finally own. Do you
know it only gets worse from here. Cash only.

"Now More Than Ever"

This is a phrase used by Whites to express their surprise and disapproval of social or political conditions which, to the Negro, are devastatingly usual. Often accompanied by an unsolicited touch on the forearm or shoulder, this expression is a favorite among the most politically liberal but socially comfortable of Whites. Its origins and implications are necessarily vague and undefined. In other words, the source moment of separation between "now" and "ever" must never be specified. In some cases it is also accompanied by a solicitation for unpaid labor from the Negro, often in the form of time, art, or an intimate and lengthy explanation of the Negro's life experiences, likely not dissimilar to a narrative the Negro has relayed before to dead ears. Otherwise, in response to the circumstances occurring "now," as ever, but suddenly and inexplicably "more" than ever, this is an utterance to be met with a solemn nod of the head and— eventually and most importantly—absolution, which all Good Whites are convinced they deserve. When a time or era achieves "more than ever" status, many Negroes will assume duties kindred to those of priesthood, e.g., receiving confessions, distributing mercy, et cetera. Although, as noted above, the precise connotation of this phrase is quite obscured in its usage, it seems to be uttered in moments of "Aha!" or, more bluntly, "I straight up did not believe you before," wherein before = "ever." (See also: Negro Lexicon entries #42 & #43: "same shit, different day" and "samo samo.") Subtexts, then, underscoring this phrase are quite sinister in nature, varying from "Your usefulness, Negro, is married to your misfortune," and "Time is linear," the implications of which are that (1) value is time sensitive, (2) conditions of despair are temporary, and (3) anything at all can be new, belonging exclusively to "now," and untethered to "ever," (i.e., past, future, world history). These understandings of time versus import are likely due to the fact that any spur to action or empathy for the White is often directly correlated to any present dangers facing their individual freedoms, or even simply when one "feels like it." (See also: Case Study #5: "Empathy.") This reveals in Whites a compulsion to reformation based upon desire, excitement, guilt, or otherwise self-indulgent emotions, whereas it would appear that the Negro must live the life of the Negro, ever, now, and ever

and ever and ever and ever and ever and ever and ever
and ever and ever and ever and ever and ever and ever
and ever and ever and ever and ever and ever and ever
and ever and ever and ever and ever and ever and ever
and ever and ever and ever and ever and ever and ever
and ever and ever and ever and ever and ever and ever
and ever and ever and ever and ever and ever and ever
and ever and ever and ever and ever and ever and ever
and ever and ever and ever and ever and ever and ever
and ever and ever and ever and ever and ever and ever
and ever and ever [. . .] and ever and ever and ever and
ever and ever and ever and ever and ever and ever and
ever and ever and ever and ever and ever and ever and
ever and ever and ever and ever and ever and ever and
ever and ever and ever and ever and ever and ever and
ever and ever and ever and ever and ever and ever and
ever and ever and ever and ever and ever and ever and
ever and ever and ever and ever and ever and ever and
ever and ever and ever and ever and ever and ever and
ever and ever and ever and ever and ever and ever and
ever and ever and ever and ever and ever and ever and
ever and ever and ever and ever and ever and ever [. . .]
and ever and ever and ever and ever and ever and ever
and ever and ever and ever and ever and ever (cont.)

Black Women for Beginners Pt. 1

Every time a hot comb simmers
we dread. We get hurt so often
we think it's a nickname.

When we say we remember

we mean hurricane, hunt,
meadow, lust, duty, escape,
settle, mourn, birch, baptism,
tithe, kneel, Sphinx, throat,
offering, animal, deadwood.

We get hurt so often we never
run. Every time we lick our lips
the day obeys and repents.

Glory glory hallelujah.
Hot comb on the stove.
Train tracks in the weeds.

When a Man I Love Jerks Off in My Bed next to Me and Falls Asleep

I think of my father
vodka-laughing: *Aw shit,*
when Daddy said go pick out a switch
from the lemon tree we knew
that switch better be good.
My father was a drunk altar boy.
My father was a southern boy.
Now my father is a good man.
When you grow up in the South, you know
the difference between a good switch and a bad one.
Pick what hurts best. The difference between drinking
to disappear and drinking to remember.
Be polite. Be gentle. Be a vessel. Be ashamed.
As a child, I begged to be whooped.
I pinched myself with my nails when I was wrong.
I tried to pull out my eyelashes. I said, *Punish me*
I said *for I have sinned I am disgusting.*
Here is the order in which we studied the Bible
in second grade: (1) Genesis, or, God is a man
and he owns you. You were bad. Put on some
got-damn clothes. (2) Exodus, or, you would still
be a slave if it were not for men. Also, magic.
Magic or, never question a man's truth.
(3) Job, or, suffer, suffer because it is holy.

During the classes on Revelation, I think
I drifted to sleep. I think I dreamed
trumpets when I touched my hot parts
then touched the cold steel of my desk.
I knew what it meant to be wrong and woman.
When I walk into the world and know
I am a black girl, I understand
I am a costume. I know the rules.
I like the pain because it makes me.
I deserve the pain. I deserve you
looking at me, moaning, looking away.
Son of a bitch. My rent is due.
No one kissed my tits and read the Bible.
Good and evil. Pleasure and empty
curtain grid of dawn light.
I call this honor. I call this birthright.

Who Were Frederick Douglass's Cousins, and Other Quotidian Black History Facts That I Wish I Learned in School

I have a body. It sits in a desk.
Every day is bitten with new guilt.
My teacher can see right
through me, all the way
to Black History Month.
It is my fortune to be
ashamed, and from nowhere.
How can I concentrate
on *photosynthesis* when
there is a thing called *Africa*?
When my teacher talks about slaves,
I become a slave. I know too much.
I raise my hand. American flag
and family tree. Is it my fault
my stomach aches? I wait
in my desk and try to be still.
I lie and immediately confess.
I grow a plant in a paper towel.
I get in trouble for talking.
At recess, I pretend.
The mountains are closing in.
I am good, but too curious.
What happened to the Indians?

How do we know about heaven,
and dragonflies?
Where did Harriet Tubman sleep?
Who did Harriet Tubman kiss?
What about the Africans that stayed?
Why are they hungry?
Did Frederick Douglass's mother
brush his hair in the morning?
Was he tender-headed and afraid?
Is this how I am supposed to feel?
Are you sure? How do you know?

A Brief History of the Present

Virgil Tibbs isn't arrested, exactly, but the white cop in
Sparta, Mississippi, tells him to spread his legs, *boy*, and
get into the back of the police car. Darren Wilson cannot
find a job, twelve months after the shooting, which left
his round cheeks pink with adrenaline. He lives a quiet
life. His blue eyes sparkle. He is a man who shot a boy.
No—a suspect. *Boy.* Rodney King became nationally
known after he was beaten. Journalists consider flimsy
words: *ironic* and *alternative, fault* and *intention.* Even
angels want L.A. fame. On the phone I ask Jericho how
the South is treating him. He says today he wasn't shot
to death, and we laugh. There's no way a black woman
killed herself, because everyone knows we can withstand
inhuman amounts of pain. (There's no way she didn't
hang herself, dumb brown martyr, not mentally sound
to begin with.) Immortal. Magical. Not like angels, but
like drinking water, like roads. Trick question: Is mercy
ever justified? Aren't all masters benevolent? Now, please
use the space below to create a graph showing the price
of water. There's no way we don't deserve it. In 1992 in
California my white classmates are like, aren't you glad
you're free. *Your people.* What if you lived in the olden
days. I've seen pictures of slavery, crude charcoals in
watered-down history books, and that's how I know I'm
not a slave. (A Sgt. testified that Rodney King exhibited

Hulk-like strength. His name was Koon, and repetition is a literary device, and paranoia is a weakness of the oppressed: we cannot be mentally sound.) What began to leak, then, from the laceration was discipline, which for the slave is a tic of survival, and for a nation is the practice of denial. What did he have in his system? Was it hunger, or money? Was it glass, plants, voice? Death is the only cultural truth, because there are fake marriages every day, and even rappers are cooked up in an office, in somebody's pink cheeks. Dylann Roof, Burger King, Urban Outfitters. I know it's just a movie, but I'm still afraid of what I see when I fall asleep. I know the masses ask me every day for a eulogy. I know I am supposed to say *shot and killed*, say *brutality*, to call my life a life. This is their language and not mine. This is not my mouth. Multiple choice: In what year did a black man hang from a tree? Who is a nigger? Which of the following are Negroes free to do: marry, own property, vote, drive, speak, bear arms, organize, revolt, be president, make movies, laugh. Which is greater: the amount of minutes it takes for requested backup to arrive at the scene of a twelve-year-old in a park playing with toys, or the varieties of insects that might make contact with a person laid in a street over the course of four hours on a summer evening in St. Louis? How patient must we be? Praise the

endurance. (Or is it suspicious, almost not human? Who
else is so great but the devil himself?) I worry sometimes
I will only be allowed a death story. No one will say in
the *New Yorker* how my mother made her money, who
I married, how my career began. *Your people.* The death
story is just a name folded into another name. My name
might be a list, or a hymn, or a body, an investigation,
a year, a lineage. I might become an autopsy, and
the reason won't matter, only my understanding, my
swallowing of my rightful place, tectonic plates clicking
like a jaw, and—stubbornly, like history—my mouth
becoming their mouth speaking who I am.

Ode to Fried Chicken's Guest Appearance on *Scandal*

Everyone likes it.
That's not the point.
In America the ocean isn't rising.
I allow the chicken
to be my stand-in.
For argument's sake, I encompass
all chicken. All guns.
The thing about guns
is everyone is dying.
That's not the point.
On *Scandal*
the white President says
gun violence.
He is fucking a black woman
secretly. That's when
the chicken enters. I take
the liberty of assessing
the chicken as such: the wedge
between someone's
forefathers, crispy hot threat
to sanctity. A monument.
Olivia's in the white coat again,
her wide collar of morality
standing for the gall of us.

Everybody wants a taste.
Everybody's dying.
Everybody wants a taste.
The chicken is sacred Black pussy.
The chicken invades your homes.
The chicken circles the truth.
The chicken can fly.
The chicken is how we riot.
The salt, the terror.
They should have never
brought us here.

Magical Negro #1: Jesus Christ

They make his eyes that color
so he can seduce you. Literally
every white boyfriend tender
until they're not. Y'all know
that nigger was a nigger.
Y'all know those whores
were whores. Sometimes
I go to the sink for water
and I come back with a jar
full of wine. Every second
I breathe, I forgive.

Matt

For all intents and purposes and because the rule applies
more often than it doesn't, every white man or boy who
has entered and fallen away from my particular moderate
life has been called Matt. Not Dan. Rarely Ben. Never
Matthew. Matt smokes unfiltered Pall Malls because Kurt
Vonnegut did. We talk on Myspace because he goes to a
different high school. Matt's in love with someone else but
I can tell he's still interested in me. Matt and his girlfriend
aren't really together. Matt doesn't have a condom so we
can't. Matt also doesn't have a condom so we can't. Matt
loves Modest Mouse. Matt loves Kanye. He loves whiskey.
He brings a flask to the park. He tells me I'm beautiful. He
likes me. He follows me into the bathroom where I once
found a bag of coke. I tip sideways onto the tile trying to
steady myself on top of him while his legs are spread on
the toilet lid. I say what about you and Anna. He says hold
your ankles. I made Matt a really good mix CD. Matt's
writing a novel. Matt's also writing a novel. Matt says
I'm a really good kisser. My friends say I'm too good for
Matt. Matt loves his mom. Matt's moving to Berlin. Matt's
moving to California. Matt's quitting smoking again. Matt
rolls his own cigarettes. Matt has depression. He listens to
sad songs. Matt wants a big family. He seems like he would
be a good dad. His family is so white. His favorite novelists
are white. His ex-girlfriends are white. He said he would
call me. His ex-girlfriends are really skinny. He has this

thing where he seems like he doesn't care about anything.
Matt's in love with someone else. He thought I was way
older than him. He got a new tattoo. He has bad dreams. I
miss him. He loves foreign movies. He's stoned all the time.
He pulls me into another room. He has a beard and he
also has a beard. He kisses me in the other room. He loves
my dog. He flirts with me all the time, I think just for fun.
Oh, Matt. He knows he's a white man but doesn't think of
himself as a white man. He doesn't know what to do with
his life. He floats. He is young. He can afford to be cool.
He wears a lot of flannel. We're just friends. He's nervous
about commitment. He's nervous in the elevator when he
touches the small of my back. He's nervous on the roof. I'm
nervous taking his hand because people can see us. His
roommate walks in on us, then gives us shots of gin we all
sip in silence. After that we smoke on his fire escape and
make out. We smoke in front of the bar and make out. We
make out on an empty subway train; my back slips around
on the hard plastic seat. He pays for my brunch. He texts
me all the time even at the airport. He's breaking up with
his girlfriend. He and his friends are drunk in someone's
apartment in Queens, what am I up to? He hates his job
but he's totally a genius. He lost his phone so he has a
new number. He hates his job and what he really wants
to do is make art and be happy. He needs to live abroad
for a while. He used to be really dumb. He swats his hair

from his forehead and says of course he will call. I always ask but I'm going to stop asking. I'm nervous he doesn't understand. He didn't grow up with many black people. He knows he is part of the problem. He just believes in love and knowledge. Matt, Matt, Matt, Matt. Each one more beautiful than the last. Each one more with more intricate ennui. I could never love him. He floats. I can't stop loving him. Matt knows the bartender. Matt studied comparative literature. He still loves his ex, I just know it. He says I like talking to you. He says watch your head as I ride him in his dorm room bunk bed. He's so sorry he didn't call, it's just that things have been busy and weird. Matt and I sneak out of a movie to hook up in his car. He is afraid of me. Matt and I are hanging out this week I think, to watch movies or something. I guess, maybe. He's never met anyone like me. Things are just super casual with us. Neither of us is looking for a relationship. Matt loves relationships. He slept with my friend. I can't tell if he's into me because I'm black or because I'm not that black and either way I feel bad. I feel it in my stomach's basement: Matt can't want me. I am not forever. Matt has kissed me hundreds of times and he kissed my ancestors, too. He held them down and kissed them real good. He was young and he could afford it. When he touched them, they always smiled, almost as if it had been rehearsed.

"Lilac Wine" by Eartha Kitt vs. "Lilac Wine" by Jeff Buckley

How many men
before I understand. I don't want to

but I do. Invade.
Try to breathe

from their mouths.
The master's tools—

I have them.
The house is getting too big.

My people—there's style,
there's misery.

The finest imports. Tender,
bittersweet. I want to

build a reef for us,
fill it with arrows.

What I Am

after Terrance Hayes

I drink the glamour
even when it makes me sick. Eleven
or Two it don't matter I'm not
lost waiting to be famous I'm
waiting in line at Walgreens
for my pills and texting
a white man I hope will fuck me.
He smells like rolling papers
and the ocean in Santa Barbara.
I consider buying chips and *Ebony*
and dog-earing every page that says
hallelujah. I keep saying I'm black
so I don't forget. I twist my hair
in my fingers and watch time go silk.
I drink the glamour and offer myself.
If I could I would fuck them all.
They don't know what I am. I play
my tarot only at night, my eyes fall,
I get mean, I fall in love, I deny this.
The supremacy makes me ache.
The supremacy calls me baby.
The people in commercials we are slowly
becoming them, biting our lips because
the taste of meat. Nothing is sexier

than how hungry I am. I say thick
means hallelujah. Size Two or Six
it don't matter the pills
are a cartoon animal, a quiet sister,
and I'm the type of girl says
same shit different day.
I call to medicine in my sleep.
I don't crash into rocks.
And everywhere I see myself
and I am a nigger girl you love.
Is it wrong that I feel nothing.
Is it wrong that I feel nothing.

If you are over staying woke

Water
the plants. Drink
plenty of water.
Don't hear
the news. Get
bored. Complain
about the weather.
Keep a corkscrew
in your purse.
Don't smile
unless you want
to. Sleep in.
Don't see the news.
Remember what
the world is like
for white people.
Listen to
cricket songs.
Floss. Take pills.
Keep an
empty mind.
When you are
hungover
do not say
I'm never drinking

again. Be honest
when you're up
to it. Otherwise
drink water
lie to yourself
turn off the news
burn the papers
skip the funerals
take pills
laugh at dumb shit
fuck people you
don't care about
use the Crock-Pot
use the juicer
use the smoothie maker
drink water
from the sky
don't think
too much about the sky
don't think about water
skip the funerals
close your eyes
whenever possible
When you toast
look everyone in the eyes

Never punctuate
the president
Write the news
Turn
into water
Water
the fire escape
Burn the paper
Crumble the letters
Instead of
hyacinths pick
hydrangeas
Water the hydrangeas
Wilt the news
White the hydrangeas
Drink the white
Waterfall the
cricket songs
Keep a song mind
Don't smile
Don't wilt
funeral
funeral

Who Speaks for the Earth?

It's 2014   I get it
I'm here but I'm not really here

When we are not pleased we proclaim
the year as if remembering suddenly

We have just counted all the tree rings in
Sequoia National Park then fallen into deep sleep

We are addicted to linear time/ Who did what
to whom when/ We use verb tenses

For example, "Chased into a white sheet"/ "Is haunting"
or, "Wasn't an angel"/ "Isn't breathing any longer"

We make a lot of trash but whatever/ There is
a particular way in which we are always in awe

It is 2014 and still   I always have bad dreams
I have been blowing in this breeze so many nights

I mourn my other selves
My stupid body in the dirt

This ritual tide   this blue myth   This
indictment   I rent

My stupid body stiffening on a dark road
My stupid body and my stupid memory

You speak/ I say the word *return*
I never learned the word *escape*

I say Oh My God/ I am speaking
to myself/ for my pleasure

It is 2014 we say we cannot believe it
Nothing belongs to me

Sometimes I'm like please please please please
I kiss my mom at the airport and kiss the soil

You speak/
I am afraid to stay here

The opposite of space is the ocean
They are both my beginning

There's this life of sage and piano
I speak   I ruin   What else

Black Ego (Original Soundtrack)

Language back then was a fly behind
my eyelid and I was getting even harder

to love. Was the cigarette falling
from my grandfather's sleeping lips,

how I still can't figure the need for saviors.
A little bit about me: Never learned

my real name, and sometimes I think
I see his fedora in the smoke I make.

The way they tell it, the sand and river
are real, and I am moving in them.

I say *You don't want any of this shit*
right here. It is easy for me to forget

about molecules. I began, which is
not the same as being uncovered.

My real name easy as prints on glass.
My real name can't help myself.

Origin was a mystic bounce. I was
never a gentle wish, so it's fair

to say I can't sit still. First bass line
settled into the wood floor of my chest

like a gasp. Here is a possible scene
from a black-and-white movie about me:

I'm a man on my couch, legs wide
and wondering, drooling wine

or Oreo crumbs into my cleavage
and shit if I ain't still alone. In the movie

I'm still poor. I boil water in sepia light.
I know a little something

another Morgan narrates *about what makes
the blues blue.* A creamy song shakes

the window like a wave. Sights just don't
do it for me anymore, and I toss back

my motionless hair as if it isn't a symbol,
as if I have swallowed Lana Turner's eyes

from a cordial glass. I keep trying
like a fool to be sincere: there are only

nails in me. I was meant to stay
hungry, to lick my own sword.

I TOLD MY THERAPIST I TRIED TO
MEDITATE AND SHE LAUGHED

I can't leave the house
bc I'm invisible/ the landscape
is like really hectic vibes/
I've been thinking/ Goddamnit
I'm trying/ to get whole/ I snake
wheat fields/ I'm obsessed
with how people are wrong/
They are ugly and so am I/
I am perfect/ bc I know
everything/ I carry a light
made out of your mouth/
Here we are/ We are sick
but/ we will not be sick forever/
I have three heads/ so
I'm perfect/ snow
at my feet/ Blood
Moon in my pussy/ Anything
good/ you can find/ in the dark

"Parker's Mood" by Charlie Parker

I am only as lonely
as anybody else, I say
at lunch downtown, examining
my worth. It isn't
summertime. At the end,

III.
POPULAR NEGRO PUNCHLINES

GREAT AMERICA

Where even in death, in miniature
carved stone, some display
in a dark hallway at the Metropolitan
Museum of Art, we never escape
the fucking guy on the street
when I'm just walking
to the gallery to meet a friend,
who could be a lover in a different
eclipse season, because this one is
about destruction, it makes you say
Stop looking at me when I ask to be
a vindication, it is about a heat wave
that drives out the sort of company
I want to write spells for, say
indefinite as if it were a word
with a real concept behind it,
as if it had any context,
as if there were any imagination
left from the fall of our stinking
expanse of sweat and dahlias and wartimes
and insects and escapes and
sinkholes and caves and patterns and jokes
and consumers
and televisions and invisible numbers
and scandals and every kind of boat

and religions and mammies and world
champions and natural disasters
and spooks and illegals and casseroles and celebrity
baby names and prizes and trophies and
wives and discounts and loans and skin
and skin-bleaching and
civil rights and McNuggets and shipping
containers and emojis and slurs and amendments
and disco albums and priests and maps
and security systems and galas
and job titles and car mufflers and good
deals and altars and defunct
social networking websites and
brothers and niggas and magazines
and grudges and watermelons and
conspiracy theories and colleges
and special editions and deluxe editions
and holocausts and relief workers
and con artists and domestic partnerships
and rubies and law firms and elegies
and Uncle Toms and neighborhoods and excuses
and police procedures and plastic bags and mosques
and raccoons and skeletons and hate groups
and negotiables and investigations and blind
dates and types of cancer and ways to

kill yourself and forms of identification and
fetishes and Bibles and consumers
and performances and wedding venues and livestock
and macchiatos and epiphanies and names,
when it could have been an otherwise easy day,
that specific fucking guy whose eyes prick
and ravage, pathetic, as he says *Nubian.*

Magical Negro #89: Michael Jackson in Blackface on a Date with Tatum O'Neal, 1970s

There, I said it: I've been thinking
about buying a gun. There's a precedent
for my kind, and it doesn't end.
My sense of time and condition is always
six months to eight years ahead, or
two days to one-hundred-fifty years behind.
To be safe, I remain in a state of repentance.
I can't help it. Our song plays in the grocery store.
I'm picking out parsnips. I imagine
telling my dad I'm buying parsnips
and laugh at the way he would say *Girl*
Don't you know you're a Negro? What
in the hell? A confession is: in this moment
I do not know precisely how parsnips taste,
only that I've had them before—some dinner party,
some New American Brooklyn situation—
and I was delighted, lifting my glass to toast
a Grüner, for no reason in particular except
I approximate myself as something to celebrate.
I could go on like this for decades. Dress-up
is what we call blessed. I only get turned on
in hiding, shoulder to door jamb and maybe
a rifle. We are scared shitless to leave the house
as ourselves, and we like it that way.

Isn't repentance always a question?
The glass is empty now. I'm desperate as Motown
snow. Something hissing in my palms.
I can never ever stop
thinking about Fred Hampton
and youth, and how it ends. Grown-up
is when the other you eats you, when
what you allow is a monster. Sometimes
in bed with white lovers, I ask permission
to show my dark. The devils underground
are still.

Guess Who's Coming to Dinner

Spencer Tracy, growing more frustrated, decides to take
a drive, in search of a particular flavor of ice cream. At
the drive-in, he tells the waitress on roller skates that he
can't remember the particular flavor of ice cream. There
are many choices available to him. Reciting each one,
the waitress on roller skates is very obviously bored by
the embarrassment of available choices. Spencer Tracy
can have whatever he wants, but he pines for the familiar
thing. He doesn't understand why anything has to change.
He lifts the white plastic spoon to his curling lips. Of the
boysenberry ice cream, he says, "This isn't the stuff." Hours
before, his daughter brought home Sidney Poitier, played
by Sidney Poitier. World-class deliverer of ultimatums,
very well-spoken, perhaps even unbelievable in his
broad-shouldered and gentle luminosity, Sidney Poitier
has granted Spencer Tracy permission to say no. Why any
objection would be reasonable is implied. Having almost
consumed both scoops of boysenberry, Spencer Tracy has
to admit it isn't half bad. The dilemma—the unfortunate
and unwavering dark sky, how in it, the crescent moon is
even more beautiful—is a point of contention and debate
for all characters, but perhaps most notably for the family's
angry, wise-cracking black cook, Tillie. She is loud and
hardened, a thing to be tolerated, and she makes the most
fantastic pies. She does not advance the plot. Katharine
Hepburn shines in this Academy Award Winning role.

My Sister Says White Supremacy Is Turning Her Crazy

Pandemic of lilies   dreaming majesty
Hovers like sweat & unwraps you & you
    are in love
        It makes you bad,   bad
            Is your name
    Is the desert
    Is movement   long kiss
heavy gut   slow
        slow hands   in your seeds

We Are the House That Holds the Table at Which Yes We Will Happily Take a Goddamn Seat

after Solange

No one can serve two masters
like we can, be future

and what they threatened to forget,
be Richard Pryor Live on Sunset

and be the sunset. Kiss the ground,
burn it to the ground, slay dragon,

speak dragon. Sometimes it feels like
we invented America ourselves.

The difference between worth
and worthless without them

is science: how it feels to not be
able to see a person, and the number

of instances when we believed
we should die. For dinner, watermelon

and a dry white. Gin nightcap,
low moon. How fucking dare we.

The probability of a wave
carrying a pearl in its mouth

is the probability of a lamb
slicing its own white neck

tying its legs to a spit
for someone else's feast.

Why the Jive Bird Sings

for Charif Shanahan

Because—come
through numb

waters, dragging rosaries
and years, mouthful

of salt and lemon
trees, galactic

plate of ash, sick
enough to face

every midnight, saw a rosebush
and it spoke, never

was desired, inherited
from planetary alignments

and congress
self-sabotage

as possible homeland,
feeling the spirit, put every mother

to sleep, swallowed every
plant in Africa, got named

Who or How because
the answer to Why is always

fear, and lack is so convenient
it swells like an oak tree—

the thing—
is not yet dead.

Magical Negro #80: Brooklyn

Here is the bright, young food co-op.
Here is the steeple. Here are the royals
not yet dead. Here are the Niggas With
Amethyst crystals. Shea butter
halos orbit half-shaved heads bowed
for vindication. Our mother patchouli
who art in the apothecary on Flatbush
hallowed be your Dutch wax dress.
Give us this day we light soy candles
for dead brothers. Give us this day we soak
our supremacy wounds.
Give us this day.
Give us fresh juice green
as avocados, and strength
to dismantle Fox News. We are marching
even in our sleep. We are reading
DuBois, getting high off the salt eaters.
Thy kingdom come to yoga. Thy will
be a black feminist Tumblr. Thy will is not
our struggle. Forgive us. We have gathered
to learn to pronounce *freedom*.
Procession body roll, communion oysters
with prosecco. Roses for our waist beads.
We have moved away from suburbia.
Now we live on Saturn.

We don't pray anymore
the way our parents taught us.
Instead we stack our arms
with wood and music
hatches from our tongue rings.
Hymns for the dead, hookahs for
the almost-dead. Praise our half-lives.
Our bodies break but we still sage them.
We wrote the good book: instructions
for building new worlds.
Lead us not into white neighborhoods.
Deliver us from microaggressions.
Blessed are we who mourn, we who
are a blood built on a hill of embers.
We no mail-order hipster black wife.
We just trying to text our moms.
We are what we eat, leafy and anointed.
We are who we serve: banquets and bouquets
forever, foreverever, foreverever.

The Black Saint & the Sinner Lady &
the Dead & the Truth

For one thing, I hate stillness. On the front porch,
waiting, I see an animal I don't recognize:

feet of a bird, wings of a leaf. The grotesqueness
of attachment, the loudness of the woods, I knew it

when I was dead before. I died for my sins
and because of this, I am in the woods now,

aching. It is June. I am used to being
a certain kind of alone. Soon my photosynthesis

will complete, and I will be the gap
between Angela Davis's teeth. Do you ever

love something so much, you become it?
Like how when hard rain comes, you learn

quick. You straighten your shoulders and hope
this is better than touching.

I say *casual death*, and the half-moon
is my enemy, an uncertain white girl.

I wish I didn't care. I am myself
shaking hands, so subtle no one notices.

Sometimes, it's my rib cage, or my throat
does the same damn thing as my skull,

the little bear inside it. Please
don't make me repeat myself.

Preface to a Twenty Volume Joke Book

And now, each night I count the stars,

And each night I get the same number.

—Amiri Baraka, "Preface to a Twenty Volume Suicide Note"

I'm done with *The Real World*
Now I watch *Top Chef*

And dream about a life of tasting
And get so hungry I could die

I don't root for the moon-face
Pale in his intention

I'm grown up
I'm rooting for the black girl

Cooking fried chicken for the first challenge
All my life I taste

"Whatever man I'm a black girl"
Shaking her afro

My feelings are pretty real
Sexism is pretty real

No one tells me I'm beautiful
I dream about tasting

In all my baby photos I have this
Look like Oh My God

I feel sorry
I have always been terrified to be

This is just a taste
It's not ready yet

Roll the token around on your tongue
And let it breathe back at you

I butter my skin
A curse I drink and drink

When I wake up I never think
I will be told to be ashamed

I'm not ashamed
No one tells me I'm beautiful

Sometimes Stevie Wonder makes me cry
There is a little chill in the air

I have seen everyone before
I say everyone

Is dying but that is not what I mean
Everyone is getting killed

Animals with long greedy tongues
Animals living on blue mountains

Literally my body
Shaped like a question mark

I am trying to get lower to the ground
I am trying to breathe the soil

I want to know the future
Whatever man I'm black

No one tells me I'm safe
I'm done with singing

The only songs I know are work songs
I'm grown up chained

To bad ideas and sugar
My bad ideas are pretty real

One of them is dark arms in the sea
While the sun comes up

I can take a headcount
I don't think anything is a mystery

I know I'm ungrateful
I know I am very hungry

I wait too long to give up
Several eclipses pass

My hands burn and peel
Everyone is corny so I'm alone

Whatever man I'm alone
Oregano leaves shrivel I'm alone

I want to know the future
is a bright violet grape

Everything has skin
Everyone tells me sorry

I know the world is dangerous
Everyone tells me sorry

I am hallelujah the first plague
My name is suitable for spitting

Please touch me
all I have

are these terrible animals
this hunger

Toward a New Theory of Negro Propaganda

On July 4, 2017, I unearth a website called NIGGERMANIA. I walk into an antique store in a liberal California town and emerge with $88 worth of mammies and golliwogs. I have names I do not know about. For example, when Sylvia Plath wrote "nigger-eye," what do you think she meant? When she said *Lazarus*, was it a noun or a verb? White propaganda operates cyclically and within its own tragic limits, reaching a linear end only to begin again at a linear starting point. White propaganda is a stutter of imagination.

The hunted must be clever. The hunted has two primary tools of survival: imagination and hyperbole. Where the White might see linearity, for example, the Negro might see reproduction. Where the Negro might see luck in a collard green, the White might see $7.99 per pound.

For example, the Negro obviously understands how the talking heads of reality TV stars are essentially a manifested rendering of the Greek chorus; how fault is assembled episode by episode; how it matters who gets named what. The Negro thinks about Greek myths quite a bit, how such stories, for all their respected antiquity in the American imagination, are sanctums of Whiteness, such that the realm of them and their reverence presumes that only Whites may be cast in multiple representations of model behaviors, while the Negro must repeat less-revered "folklore" on an endless and aching loop. White propaganda relies upon the unwavering belief that any versions of nirvana require the absence of the Negro. This is both the conscious and unconscious peak of White Imagination.

Of course, the feedback loop of Sambo and Panther fables is inescapable only if the Negro concedes to internalize the mythology of the White (and as such, the imagination of the White, and as such, the latent desire for the Negro's own demolition) as Standard. It is therefore in the Negro's best interest to learn the language and rhetoric of the White and use the fluency to their advantage in matters of not only self-preservation, but also self-recognition.

The Negro is suspicious of the laugh track, and any rhetoric or imagery that inherently denies the space of the Negro body. The Negro is suspicious, and they ought to be, lest the Negro begin to render themselves invisible, inferior, and unbeautiful in their own imaginations.

Case study: Closing a window, a young Negro woman sees a police car idling in front of her apartment building and thinks *What did I do wrong?* A young white woman has called the police. It is possible that in the dark slumbering of their unconscious, the White imagines that the only remedy for fear is death.

Negro propaganda is born of the opportunity in blips, dead air, revision, imploding narratives, and space travel. Negro propaganda at its best should seek to play the Offense as opposed to the Defense, and *really go out there and give one hundred and ten percent,* as it were. Negro propaganda insists upon simultaneity, the incongruent and antithetical, continuity only by way of a freestyled repetition. The Negro is Nevertheless. Here go the Negro, hanging roses to dry in the archways.

One example of successful Negro propaganda is the song "Grillz," from Nelly's album *Sweatsuit,* on the cover of which our hero grabs his crotch determinately. In the beginning, a scenario is proposed wherein the listener is encouraged to hold up a jewelry store and, in lieu of paper money, demand a custom-made dental apparatus constructed with diamonds and rose gold. (*Why are there so many luxury cars in the hood?*) Of another such instance of supply and demand, it is said that, when paired, the colors yellow and red, as signifiers within a landscape of White propagandist imagery, will stimulate insatiable hunger. (*But do you have McDonald's money?*)

The Negro is not good with money, but why should mathematics be applied to something as precious as flesh? Why should the Negro be good with money when the Negro is always getting sold?

The Negro imagines a flood, and another flood, and endlessness, a limitless Negro Imagination.

Angela Bassett with a match & the gap between Malcolm X's teeth & Frederick Douglass's side part & Dave Chappelle in Africa & Lil Uzi Vert & the gap between James Baldwin's teeth & the gap between Angela Davis's teeth & imagine possible homelands & refusal is not inaction & protest is not palatable & who got the keys to my Jeep & the church parking lot & the measured size of our skulls & leave my body alone & only Judge Joe Brown can judge me & back in the day & a joke about my hair & Diana Ross eating a rib & Harriet Tubman's face & laugh track & laugh track

Laugh Track Laugh Track Laugh Track Laugh Track
Regular Black Regular Black Nigger I Nigger I Black   We
till soil   We murdered

for capital   We ride around shining
in our own wake   We even make chains look good

IT WAS SUMMER NOW AND THE COLORED PEOPLE CAME OUT INTO THE SUNSHINE

They descend from the boat two by two. The gap in
Angela Davis's teeth speaks to the gap in James Baldwin's
teeth. The gap in James Baldwin's teeth speaks to the
gap in Malcolm X's Teeth. The gap in Malcolm X's teeth
speaks to the gap in Malcolm X's teeth. The gap in
Condoleezza Rice's teeth doesn't speak. Martin Luther
King Jr. Boulevard kisses the Band-Aid on Nelly's cheek.
Frederick Douglass's side part kisses Nikki Giovanni's
Thug Life tattoo. The choir is led by Whoopi Goldberg's
eyebrows. The choir is led by Will Smith's flat top.
The choir loses its way. The choir never returns home.
The choir sings funeral instead of wedding, sings funeral
instead of allegedly, sings funeral instead of help, sings
Black instead of grace, sings Black as knucklebone,
mercy, junebug, sea air. It is time for war.

Acknowledgements

Thank you to the editors who first published versions of these poems in their pages:

Spook: "The History of Black People"

Hyperallergic: "Black Ego (Original Sound Track)"

Paperbag: "Everything Will Be Taken Away" and "Ode to Fried Chicken's Guest Appearance on *Scandal*"

PEN American: "Magical Negro #84: The Black Body," "Two White Girls in the African Braid Shop on Marcy and Fulton"

Lenny: "Magical Negro #3: The Strong Black Woman" "Magical Negro #217: Diana Ross Finishing a Rib in Alabama, 1990s"

Gulf Coast: "When a Man I Love Jerks Off in My Bed Next to Me and Falls Asleep"

6x6: "I TOLD MY THERAPIST I TRIED TO MEDITATE AND SHE LAUGHED"

Powderkeg: "Who Speaks for the Earth?"

Apogee Journal Online: "I Feel Most Colored When I Am Thrown Against a Sharp White Background"

February, an anthology: "What I Am"

Poetry: "If you are over staying woke" "My Sister Says White Supremacy Is Turning Her Crazy"

Sixth Finch: "Matt"

The Awl: "Preface to a Twenty Volume Joke Book"

Columbia Poetry Journal: "And Cold Sunset" and "Nancy Meyers and My Dream of Whiteness"

The Paris Review: "The High Priestess of Soul's Sunday Morning Visit to the Wall of Respect" and "Now More Than Ever"

Harper's: "The Black Saint & The Sinner Lady & The Dead & The Truth"

The Nation: "We Are the House That Holds the Table at Which Yes We Will Happily Take a Goddamn Seat"

FADER: "Magical Negro #89: Michael Jackson in Blackface on a Date with Tatum O'Neal, 1970s"

Electric Literature: "Magical Negro #607: Gladys Knight on the 200th Episode of The Jeffersons"

BuzzFeed: "Magical Negro #80: Brooklyn"

LitHub: "A Brief History of the Present"

The Wide Shore: "Let's Get Some Better Angels at This Party"

The Rumpus:"Magical Negro #1: Jesus Christ", "'Lilac Wine' by Eartha Kitt vs. 'Lilac Wine' by Jeff Buckley" and "'Parker's Mood' by Charlie Parker"

Boulevard Magazine: "Great America"

Poets.org: "IT WAS SUMMER NOW AND THE COLORED PEOPLE CAME OUT INTO THE SUNSHINE"

"Toward a New Theory of Negro Propaganda" was originally written for the *Speech/Acts* Exhibition Catalog, published by the Institute of Contemporary Art, University of Pennsylvania and Futurepoem.

"Who Were Frederick Douglass's Cousins, and Other Quotidian Black History Facts That I Wish I Learned in School" was written for a pamphlet published by The Academy for Teachers.

"Black Women for Beginners Pt. 1" was written for Rachel Eliza Griffiths' project *skin act shadows*.

Thank you to my glorious literary agents, Dan Kirschen and Tina Dubois, as well as Tamara and Andrianna and Berni and Laura Gordon and the whole ICM team, for working tirelessly for and with my every whim. I couldn't be happier to have you all on Team MP. I'm dumb with gratefulness for everyone at Tin House for always making me feel at home, especially Tony Perez, Matthew Dickman, Sabrina Wise, Nanci McCloskey, Jakob Vala, and Lance Cleland.

To my mom and dad, thank you. To my stronger sister Angel Nafis, thank you. To my life partner in crime, Tommy Pico, thank you. To the Noah Baumbach to my Wes Anderson, Vivian Lee, thank you. To The Husbands—Charif Shanahan, Nate Marshall, Danez Smith, Rob Ostrom, Jay Deshpande, Jerriod A. H. Avant, Jeremy Michael Clark, José Guadalupe Olivarez, Jayson P. Smith, Matt Nelson, Willie Fitzgerald, Sasha Fletcher, Sam Ross—thank you. There aren't enough words. I am grateful in every moment that you love me.

To my dearests, for their genius and laughter and generosity— Clea Litewka, Leah Feuer, Abba Belgrave, Alex Dimitrov, Saeed Jones, Jenna Wortham, Kimberly R. Drew, Eve L. Ewing, Fatimah Ashgar, Sam Sax, Natalie Eilbert, Molly Rose Quinn, DeLana R. A. Dameron, Nicole Sealey, Shira Erlichman, Mahoghany L. Browne, Diamond Sharp, Matt Rohrer, Thomas Parker, Meg and Tiona and Kameelah and the whole Speech/Acts team, Chanelle Aponte Pearson, Ryann Holmes, Shanté Cozier, Issisa Komada-John, Hanif Abdurraquib, Adam Dalva, Lizzie Harris, Julie Buntin, Sean Shearer, Patricia Smith, Natalie Diaz, Jami Attenberg, Karen Russell, Tracy K. Smith, SA Smythe, Camonghne Felix, Matthew Zapruder, Harmony Holiday, Mike Matesich, Nicole Counts, Margo Jefferson—I could go on forever—thank you for keeping me alive in all the endless ways you do.

To all Black people, thank you.